simple PLEASURES

Vickie Phelps

A DayMaker Greeting Book

Retirement means...

Thinking of you today, and wishing you

all the simple pleasures of life

and the time in which to enjoy them.

■ ■ ■

simple things like. . .

fiery sunsets

■ ■ ■

fleecy clouds

■ ■ ■

wind rustling
through the trees

■ ■ ■

the scent of rain

■ ■ ■

cool ocean
breezes

■ ■ ■

rainbows

■ ■ ■

fresh-baked bread

∎∎∎

early morning

solitude

∎∎∎

learning Italian

fruit from your own tree

∎∎∎

newborn colts in pasture

■ ■ ■

a baby's
innocence

■ ■ ■

conversation with
a good friend

■ ■ ■

a Sunday afternoon nap

∎ ∎ ∎

fresh-brewed

coffee

∎ ∎ ∎

evenings on the front porch

∎ ∎ ∎

on Leader Road
or Rt 89

a star-studded sky

■ ■ ■

the purr of a cat

■ ■ ■

the cicada's song

■ ■ ■

on Leader Road
Rt 89

iced tea in summer

∎∎∎

holding hands

∎∎∎

a good book
∎∎∎
in pure Italian

fresh-cut flowers

*butterflies
on the wing*

birds singing

homemade ice cream

■ ■ ■

children
laughing

■ ■ ■

fireflies

■ ■ ■

*the unconditional
love of a dog*
Luna

■ ■ ■

laughter with a friend
■ ■ ■

a favorite song
■ ■ ■
on the accordian

dew-kissed mornings

∎∎∎

autumn leaves

∎∎∎

country drives

∎∎∎

a steaming cup of tea

•••

a crackling
fireplace

•••

chocolate chip cookies
fresh from the oven

•••

starry twilight

■ ■ ■

*watermelon
in August*

■ ■ ■

a walk in the woods
with Marlene

bubble baths

▪▪▪

fluffy towels

▪▪▪

lavender-scented linens

▪▪▪

family reunions

■ ■ ■

old photos

■ ■ ■

Grandfather's stories

■ ■ ■

You will be the grandfather!

giant snowflakes

■ ■ ■

*hot chocolate
in winter*

■ ■ ■

warm, feathery comforters

■ ■ ■

a rushing
mountain
stream

■ ■ ■

a pastel sunrise

■ ■ ■

wildflowers

■ ■ ■

birthday cards

∎∎∎

candlelight

∎∎∎

beautiful

packages

∎∎∎

Sunday morning hymns

■ ■ ■

fresh garden vegetables

from Kathy's garden

■ ■ ■

lush green lawns

■ ■ ■

crisp, fall mornings

a harvest moon

pumpkins

cardinals in winter

■ ■ ■

neighborhood
snowmen

■ ■ ■

warm mittens

■ ■ ■

picnics

∎∎∎

fireworks

∎∎∎

marching bands

∎∎∎

porch swings

■ ■ ■

roasting marshmallows

■ ■ ■

campfire songs

■ ■ ■

moonlight

■ ■ ■

night sounds

■ ■ ■

star constellations

■ ■ ■

hummingbirds at the feeder

■ ■ ■

*birds building
a nest*

■ ■ ■

bees on the flowers

■ ■ ■

gentle spring rain

- - -

the first crocus
blooming

- - -

sunshine after a storm

- - -

Thou art worthy, O Lord, to receive glory and honour and
power: for thou hast created all things, and for thy pleasure
they are and were created.

REVELATION 4:11

© 2004 by Barbour Publishing, Inc.

ISBN 1-59310-200-3

Designed by Robyn Martins

All rights reserved. No part of this publication may be reproduced or transmitted in any form or by any means without written permission of the publisher.

Scripture quotations are taken from the King James Version of the Bible.

Published by Barbour Publishing, Inc., P.O. Box 719, Uhrichsville, Ohio 44683. www.barbourbooks.com

Our mission is to publish and distribute inspirational products offering exceptional value and biblical encouragement to the masses.

Printed in China.
5 4 3 2 1